CROCHET

Eternity Shawls

Designs by Jennifer McClain

General Information

Many of the products used in this pattern book can be purchased from local craft, fabric and variety stores, or from the Annie's Attic Needlecraft Catalog *(see Customer Service information on page 15).*

Autumn Hues

SKILL LEVEL

EASY

FINISHED SIZE
6 inches wide x 76 inches long before sewing seam

MATERIALS
❑ Red Heart Symphony medium (worsted) weight yarn (3½ oz/ 100g/310 yds per skein):
   2 oz each moss green #4626 *(A)* and persimmon #4906 *(B)*
❑ Landscapes by Lion Brand (1¾ oz/50 yds per skein):
   60 yds autumn trails multi #275 *(C)*
   50 yds country sunset multi #277 *(D)*
❑ Size M/13/9mm crochet hook or size needed to obtain gauge
❑ Tapestry needle

GAUGE
With C (worked in back lps only): 2 sc = 1 inch; 2 sc rows = 1 inch

INSTRUCTIONS
SHAWL
Row 1: With C, ch 150, sc in 2nd ch from hook, sc in each rem ch across. Fasten off, leaving 7-inch length for finishing. Turn. *(149 sc)*
Row 2: Join 1 strand each A and B held tog with a sl st in **back lp**

(see Stitch Guide) only of first sc; working in back lps only this row, ch 1, sc in same sc as joining, sc in each rem sc across, turn.

Row 3: Ch 1, sc in each sc across. Fasten off, leaving 7-inch length for finishing. Turn.

Row 4: Join D with a sl st in back lp only of first sc, rep row 2. Fasten off, leaving 7-inch length for finishing. Turn.

Rows 5 & 6: Rep rows 2 and 3.

Row 7: With C, rep row 4.

Rows 8 & 9: Rep rows 2 and 3.

Row 10: Rep row 4.

Rows 11 & 12: Rep rows 2 and 3.

Row 13: Rep row 7.

FINISHING

With tapestry needle and lengths left for finishing, weave ends of shawl tog to form ring. ❑❑

Evergreen Lace

SKILL LEVEL

EASY

FINISHED SIZE

8½ inches wide x 90 inches long before sewing seam

MATERIALS

❑ TLC Amore medium (worsted) weight yarn (6 oz/170g per skein):
  12 oz dark thyme #3628
❑ Size K/10½/6.5mm crochet hook or size needed to obtain gauge
❑ Tapestry needle

GAUGE

8 dc = 3 inches; 4 dc rows = 3 inches

INSTRUCTIONS

SHAWL

First half

Row 1: Ch 239 (foundation ch), ch 3 (turning ch-3), dc in fourth ch from hook, dc in each rem ch across, turn. (240 dc, counting turning ch-3 as first dc)

Row 2: Ch 1, sc in first dc, [ch 3, sk next dc, sc in next dc] across to last dc, sc in last dc, turn. (119 ch-3 sps, 121 sc)

Row 3: Ch 1, sc in first sc, [ch 1, sk next sc, sc in next sp] across to last sp, sc in last sc, turn. (121 sc, 119 ch-1 sps)

Row 4: Ch 1, sc in first sc, [ch 3, sk next sc, sc in next sp] across to last sp, sc in last sc, turn. (121 sc, 119 ch-3 sps)

Row 5: Rep row 3.

Row 6: Ch 3 (counts as first dc throughout), dc in each sc and ch-1 sp across, turn. (240 dc)

Row 7: Ch 3, dc in each rem dc across, turn.

Row 8: Ch 1, sc in first dc, ch 3, sk next dc, [sc in next dc, ch 3, sk next dc] across to last 2 dc, **sc dec** (see Stitch Guide) in last 2 dc, turn. Fasten off.

2nd Half

Row 9: Working in rem lps of foundation ch at base of row 1, join yarn with a sl st in first rem lp, ch 3, dc in each rem ch across, turn. (240 dc)

Rows 10–16: Rep rows 2–8. At end of row 16, fasten off, leaving long length for finishing.

FINISHING

With tapestry needle and length left for finishing, weave ends of shawl tog to form ring. ❑❑

Faux Hairpin Lace

FINISHED SIZE
12 inches wide x 35 inches long

MATERIALS
- ❏ Red Heart Lustersheen fine (sport) weight yarn (4 oz/113g/ 335 yds per skein):
  - 6 oz natural #0805 *(A)*
- ❏ Moda-Dea Prima bulky (chunky) weight eyelash yarn (1¾ oz/ 50g/72 yds per skein):
  - 1½ oz natural #3259 *(B)*
- ❏ Size K/10½/6.5mm crochet hook or size needed to obtain gauge

GAUGE
6 lps in pattern = 5 inches; strip = 3¾ inches wide

SPECIAL STITCH
Cross-stitch (cross-st): Sk next st, dc in next st; working over dc just made, dc in skipped st.

INSTRUCTIONS
STRIP
Make 3

Foundation row: With A, ch 4, dc in 4th ch from hook, turn, [ch 3, dc in dc, turn] 88 times. *(89 lps)*

First half
Rnd 1: Ch 1, 3 sc in first lp, [2 sc in next lp, 3 sc in next lp] across, join with sl st in first sc, turn. *(223 sc)*

Rnd 2 (RS): Ch 3 *(counts as first dc)*, [**cross-st** *(see Special Stitches)*] around, join with sl st in third ch of beg ch-3, turn. *(111 cross-sts, 1 dc)*

Rnd 3: Ch 1, sc in same st as joining, [ch 1, sk next dc, sc in next dc] around, join with sl st in first sc, turn. *(223 sc)*

Rnds 4 & 5: Ch 1, sc in same st as joining, [ch 1, sk next sc, sc in next sp] around, join with sl st in first sc, turn. At end of rnd 5, fasten off.

2nd Half
Rnd 1: With RS facing, join A with a sl st in first lp on opposite side of foundation row, rep rnd 1 of First Half.

Rnds 2–5: Rep rnds 2–5 of First Half.

JOINING STRIPS
Holding first 2 Strips with WS tog, working through both thicknesses at once, join B with a sl st in any sc, ch 1, sc in same st, [ch 1, sk next st, sc in next st] around, join with sl st in first sc. Fasten off.

Rep with 3rd Strip.

EDGING
With RS facing, join B with a sl st in any sc on either outer edge of shawl, ch 1, sc in same st, [ch 1, sk next st, sc in next st] around, join with sl st in first sc. Fasten off.

Rep on rem outer edge of shawl. ❏❏

Coconut

SKILL LEVEL

INTERMEDIATE

FINISHED SIZE

8 inches wide x 82 inches long before sewing seam

MATERIALS

❑ TLC Macaroon super bulky (super chunky) weight yarn (3 oz/85g/115 yds per skein):
  5 oz coconut #9316 *(A)*
❑ Caron Cozi bulky (chunky) weight yarn:
  3 oz sandstone #0001 *(B)*
❑ Simply Soft (medium) worsted (3 oz per skein):
  3 oz bone #2604 *(C)*
❑ Aunt Lydia's Shimmer Fashion fine (sport) weight yarn (2 oz/ 56.7g/124 yds per ball):
  2 oz light linen #2242 *(D)*
❑ Size M/13/9mm crochet hook or size needed to obtain gauge
❑ Tapestry needle
❑ Safety pin or other small marker

GAUGE

With A: 2 sc = 1 inch; 2 sc rows = 1 inch

PATTERN NOTE

To change color in single crochet, work last single crochet before color change as follows: insert hook in next stitch, yarn over with working color, draw up a loop, drop working color to wrong side, yarn over with next color, complete single crochet.

INSTRUCTIONS

SHAWL

Row 1 (WS): With A, ch 164, sc in 2nd ch from hook, [sk next ch, 2 sc in next ch] across, turn. *(163 sc)*

Row 2: Ch 1, sc in first sc, [sk next sc, 2 sc in next sc] across, turn.

Row 3: Rep row 2, **changing color** *(see Stitch Guide)* to B in last sc, turn. Do not fasten off A.

Row 4: With B, rep row 2, remove hook from lp at end of row and attach marker to hold in place. Do not turn.

Row 5: With A, draw up a lp in first sc, rep row 2, remove hook from lp at end of row and insert marker in lp, turn.

Row 6: With 1 strand each B and D held tog, rep row 2. Fasten off B, leaving 8-inch length for finishing. Turn.

Row 7: With 1 strand each C and D held tog, rep row 2. Fasten off C and D, leaving 8-inch lengths for finishing. Turn.

Row 8: Pick up dropped lp of A, rep row 2.

Rows 9–17: Rep rows 2–8 consecutively, ending with row 3. At end of row 17, do not change to B in last sc. Fasten off, leaving 8-inch length for finishing.

FINISHING

With tapestry needle and lengths left for finishing, weave ends of shawl tog to form ring. ❑❑

Plaid Pleasure

SKILL LEVEL

INTERMEDIATE

FINISHED SIZE
11 inches wide x 73 inches long before sewing seam

MATERIALS
❑ Red Heart Symphony medium (worsted) weight yarn (3½ oz/ 100g/310 yds per skein):
   5 oz each persimmon #4906 (A), juniper #4902 (B) and mystic purple #4903 (C)
❑ Size M/13/9mm crochet hook or size needed to obtain gauge
❑ Tapestry needle

GAUGE
7 sc = 3 inches; 7 sc rows = 3 inches

PATTERN NOTES
When working from chart, read all wrong side (odd-numbered) rows from left to right, all right side (even-numbered rows) from right to left.

To **change color** (see Stitch Guide) in single crochet, work last single crochet before color change as follows: insert hook in next stitch, yarn over with working color, draw up a loop, drop working color to wrong side, yarn over with next color, complete single crochet.

When changing colors at beginning or end of row, leave 7-inch length for fringe.

When joining new color in the middle of the row, leave an 18-inch length of new color for finishing. When working next row, carry 18-inch length across wrong side of work, working over it with color in use until end of row, then fasten off color that was carried, leaving a 7-inch length for fringe.

When joining new color in middle of the row, carry color to be dropped across wrong side of work, working over it with color in use until end of row, then fasten off color to be dropped, leaving a 7-inch length for fringe.

INSTRUCTIONS
SHAWL
Row 1 (WS): With B, ch 25, sc in 2nd ch from hook, sc in each of next 6 chs, changing to A in last sc, work 10 sc in A, changing to C in last sc, work rem 7 sc in C, turn. (24 sc)

Rows 2–86: Work from chart.

Rows 87–172: Beg with row 1 of chart, work from chart through row 86. At end of row 172, fasten off.

FINISHING
Fringe
Matching colors to ends of rows being worked, cut 11-inch length of yarn for each fringe. Fold length in half. Insert hook from WS to RS in end of row being worked, draw folded end of fringe through to form lp, draw loose ends of fringe and 7-inch length left for finishing, if present, through lp. Pull to tighten. Rep across both long ends of shawl. Trim fringe evenly.

Joining Ends
With tapestry needle and length of B, sew bottom of row 1 and top of row 172 tog to form ring. ❑❑

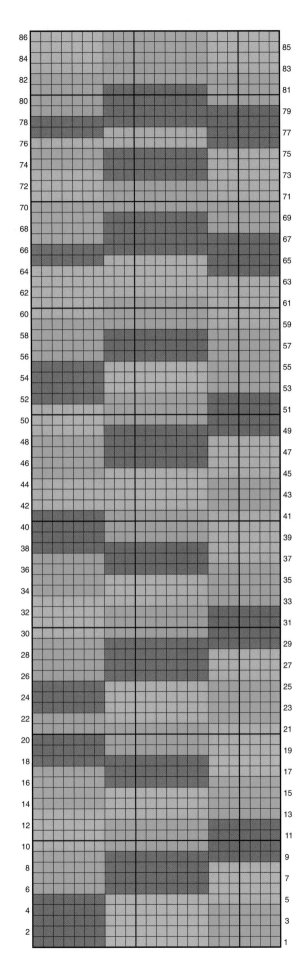

COLOR KEY
- Juniper
- Persimmon
- Mystical Purple

Shells

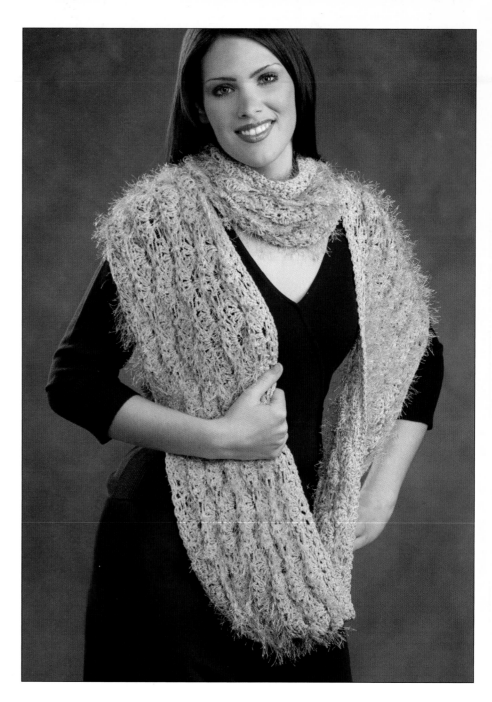

SKILL LEVEL

INTERMEDIATE

FINISHED SIZE

12 inches wide x 82 inches long before sewing seam

MATERIALS

❑ Paton's Katrina medium (worsted) weight yarn:
   13 oz oyster #10010 *(A)*
❑ Lion Brand Fun Fur Prints bulky (chunky) weight eyelash yarn (1½ oz/40g/57 yds per ball):
   3 oz sand stone multi #205 *(B)*
❑ Size M/13/9mm crochet hook or size needed to obtain gauge
❑ Tapestry needle
❑ Safety pin or other small marker

GAUGE

With A: [Shell, sc] 3 times = 8 inches

SPECIAL STITCHES

Shell: 5 dc in indicated st.
Beginning half shell (beg half shell): [Ch 3, 2 dc] in indicated st.
End half shell: 3 dc in indicated st.

INSTRUCTIONS
SHAWL

Row 1: With A, ch 182, sc in 2nd ch from hook, sc in each rem ch across, turn. *(181 sc)*

Row 2: Ch 1, sc in first sc, [sk next 2 sc, **shell** *(see Special Stitches)* in next sc, sk next 2 sc, sc in next sc] across, turn. *(30 shells)*

Row 3: Beg half shell *(see Special Stitches)* in first sc, sc in center dc of next shell, [shell in next sc, sc in center dc of next shell] across to last shell, **end half shell** *(see Special Stitches)* in last sc. Remove hook from lp and insert safety pin or other marker. Do not fasten off. Do not turn.

Row 4: Join B with a sl st in top of turning ch-3, ch 1, sc in same st, sc in each rem st across. Fasten off B. Turn. *(181 sc)*

Row 5: Pick up dropped lp of A, ch 1, sc in first sc, [sk next 2 sc, shell in next sc, sk next 2 sc, sc in next sc] across, turn. *(30 shells)*

Rows 6–20: Rep rows 3–5 consecutively 5 times.

Row 21: Ch 3 *(counts as first dc)*, [hdc in next st, sc in next st, sl st in next st, sc in next st, hdc in next st, dc in next st] across, turn. *(181 sts)*

Row 22: Ch 1, sl st in first st, [ch 1, sl st in next st] across. Fasten off, leaving 8-inch length for finishing.

Row 23: Working in rem lps across foundation ch at base of row 1, join A with a sl st in first rem lp, [ch 1, sl st in next rem lp] across. Fasten off, leaving long length for finishing.

FINISHING

With tapestry needle and length left for finishing, weave ends of shawl tog to form ring. ❑❑

Spring Blooms

SKILL LEVEL

INTERMEDIATE

FINISHED SIZE

10 inches wide x 80 inches long before sewing seam

MATERIALS

❑ Royal Fashion Crochet crochet cotton size 3 (150 yds/137m per ball):

900 yds bridal white #0926 *(A)*

300 yds each tan #0377 *(B)*, lime #0264 *(C)* and tangerine #0325 *(D)*

❑ Size K/10½/6.5mm crochet hook or size needed to obtain gauge

❑ Tapestry needle

GAUGE

With 2 strands A held tog: 3 sc = 1 inch; 3 sc rows = 1 inch

SPECIAL STITCH

Puff stitch (puff st): Draw up a lp in next sc, [yo, draw up a lp] 3 times in next sp, yo, draw through all 8 lps on hook.

INSTRUCTIONS

SHAWL

Row 1: With 2 strands A held tog, ch 248, sc in 2nd ch from hook, [ch 2, sk next 2 chs, sc in next ch] across, turn. *(83 sc, 82 ch-2 sps)*

Rows 2 & 3: Ch 1, sc in first sc, [ch 2, sk next sp, sc in next sc] across, turn.

Row 4: Ch 1; beg in first sc, [**puff st** *(see Special Stitch)*, ch 2] across to last sc, sc in last sc, turn. *(82 puff sts)*

Row 5: Ch 1, sc in first sc, [ch 2, sc in next puff st] across. Fasten off A, leaving 8-inch length for finishing. Turn. *(83 sc, 82 ch-2 sps)*

Row 6: Join 2 strands B held tog with a sl st in first sc, rep row 2. Turn.

Rows 7 & 8: Rep rows 2 and 3. At end

of row 8, fasten off, leaving 8-inch length for finishing. Turn.

Row 9: With 2 strands C held tog, rep row 6. Fasten off, leaving 8-inch length for finishing. Turn.

Row 10: Join 2 strands D held tog with a sl st in first sc, rep row 4. Fasten off, leaving 8-inch length for finishing. Turn.

Row 11: Rep row 9. Turn.

Row 12: With 2 strands A held tog, rep row 6. Turn.

Rows 13–23: Rep rows 2–12 consecutively. At end of row 23, do not fasten off. Turn.

Rows 24–29: Rep rows 2–7 with A

only; do not change colors. At end of row 29, do not fasten off. Turn.

Row 30: Ch 1, sl st in first sc, [ch 1, sl st] in each ch st and sc across. Fasten off, leaving 8-inch length for finishing.

Row 31: Working in rem lps across foundation ch at base of row 1, join A with a sl st in first rem lp, [ch 1, sl st in next rem lp] across. Fasten off, leaving 8-inch length for finishing.

FINISHING

With tapestry needle and lengths left for finishing, weave ends of shawl tog to form ring. ❑❑

Mystic Tweed

SKILL LEVEL

INTERMEDIATE

FINISHED SIZE
6 inches wide x 72 inches long before sewing seam

MATERIALS
- ❑ Red Heart Tweed medium (worsted) weight yarn (4 oz/ 113g per skein):
  - 3 oz charcoal #7079 *(A)*
- ❑ Red Heart Symphony worsted weight yarn:
  - 1 oz mystic purple #4903 *(B)*
- ❑ Moda-Dea Caché bulky (chunky) weight yarn:
  - 4 oz wink multi #2347 *(C)*
- ❑ Size M/13/9mm crochet hook or size needed to obtain gauge
- ❑ Tapestry needle

GAUGE
With 1 strand A and 1 strand B held tog, [{hdc, ch 1} 3 times, hdc] = 3 inches; 3 hdc rows = 2 inches

SPECIAL STITCHES
Extended single crochet (esc): Insert hook in indicated st, yo, draw up a lp, yo, draw though 1 lp on hook, yo, draw through 2 lps on hook.

Reverse single crochet (rev sc): Work sc from left to right.

INSTRUCTIONS
SHAWL
First Section
Row 1: With 1 strand each A and B held tog, ch 180 for foundation ch, ch 2 *(turning ch-2)*, hdc in 3rd ch from hook, [ch 1, sk next ch, hdc in next ch] across to last ch, hdc in last ch, turn. *(92 hdc, counting turning ch-2 as first hdc; 89 ch-1 sps)*

Row 2: Ch 3 *(counts as first hdc, ch-1 throughout)*, sk next hdc, hdc in next sp, [ch 1, sk next hdc, hdc in next sp] across to last sp, ch 1, sk next hdc, hdc in 2nd ch of turning ch-2, turn. *(91 hdc, 90 ch-1 sps)*

Row 3: Ch 2 *(counts as first hdc),* hdc in next sp, [ch 1, sk next hdc, hdc in next sp] across, ending with ch 1, hdc in turning ch-3 sp, hdc in 2nd ch of turning ch-3, turn. Fasten off B only, leaving 8-inch length for finishing. *(92 hdc, 89 ch-1 sps)*

Row 4: With A only, ch 1, sc in each hdc and in each ch across, turn. Fasten off A, leaving 8-inch length for finishing. *(181 sc)*

Row 5: Join C with a sl st in first sc, ch 3, sk next sc, [**esc** *(see Special Stitches)* in next sc, ch 1, sk next sc] across to last sc, hdc in last sc, turn. *(90 ch-1 sps)*

Row 6: Ch 3, [sk next sp, esc in next esc, ch 1] across to last esc, hdc in 2nd ch of turning ch-3, turn. Fasten off, leaving 8-inch length for finishing.

Row 7: Join A with a sl st in first hdc, ch 1, sc in same hdc, sc in next sp, sc in each esc and in each ch sp across, ending with sc in turning ch-3 sp, sc in 2nd ch of turning ch-2, do not turn.

Row 8: Ch 1, **rev sc** *(see Special Stitches)* across, turn. Fasten off, leaving 8-inch length for finishing.

Second Section

Row 9: Working in rem lps of foundation ch at base of row 1, join A with a sl st in first ch, ch 1, sc in same rem lp, sc in each rem lp across, turn. Fasten off, leaving 8-inch length for finishing. *(181 sc)*

Rows 10–13: Rep rows 5–8 of First Section.

FINISHING

With tapestry needle and lengths left for finishing, weave ends of shawl tog to form ring. ❑❑

306 East Parr Road
Berne, IN 46711
© 2005 Annie's Attic

TOLL-FREE ORDER LINE or to request a free catalog (800) LV-ANNIE (800) 582-6643
Customer Service (800) AT-ANNIE (800) 282-6643, **Fax** (800) 882-6643
Visit www.AnniesAttic.com

ISBN: 1-59635-046-6
Printed in USA
1 2 3 4 5 6 7 8 9

Stitch Guide

ABBREVIATIONS

beg	begin/beginning
bpdc	back post double crochet
bpsc	back post single crochet
bptr	back post treble crochet
CC	contrasting color
ch	chain stitch
ch-	refers to chain or space previously made (i.e. ch-1 space)
ch sp	chain space
cl	cluster
cm	centimeter(s)
dc	double crochet
dec	decrease/decreases/decreasing
dtr	double treble crochet
fpdc	front post double crochet
fpsc	front post single crochet
fptr	front post treble crochet
g	gram(s)
hdc	half double crochet
inc	increase/increases/increasing
lp(s)	loop(s)
MC	main color
mm	millimeter(s)
oz	ounce(s)
pc	popcorn
rem	remain/remaining
rep	repeat(s)
rnd(s)	round(s)
RS	right side
sc	single crochet
sk	skip(ped)
sl st	slip stitch
sp(s)	space(s)
st(s)	stitch(es)
tog	together
tr	treble crochet
trtr	triple treble
WS	wrong side
yd(s)	yard(s)
yo	yarn over

Chain—ch: Yo, pull through lp on hook.

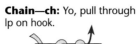

Slip stitch—sl st: Insert hook in st, yo, pull through both lps on hook.

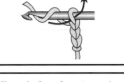

Single crochet—sc: Insert hook in st, yo, pull through st, yo, pull through both lps on hook.

Front loop—front lp
Back loop—back lp

Front Loop   Back Loop

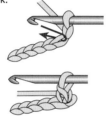

Front post stitch—fp: Back post stitch—bp: When working post st, insert hook from right to left around post st on previous row.

Back   Front

Post of Stitch

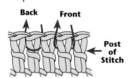

Half double crochet—hdc: Yo, insert hook in st, yo, pull through st, yo, pull through all 3 lps on hook.

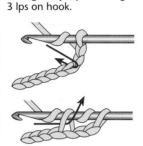

Double crochet—dc: Yo, insert hook in st, yo, pull through st, [yo, pull through 2 lps] twice.

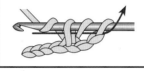

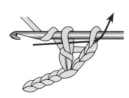

Change colors: Drop first color; with second color, pull through last 2 lps of st.

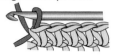

Treble crochet—tr: Yo twice, insert hook in st, yo, pull through st, [yo, pull through 2 lps] 3 times.

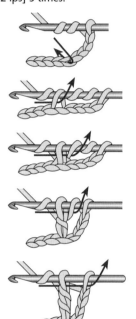

Double treble crochet—dtr: Yo 3 times, insert hook in st, yo, pull through st, [yo, pull through 2 lps] 4 times.

Single crochet decrease (sc dec): (Insert hook, yo, draw up a lp) in each of the sts indicated, yo, draw through all lps on hook.

Example of 2-sc dec

Half double crochet decrease (hdc dec): (Yo, insert hook, yo, draw lp through) in each of the sts indicated, yo, draw through all lps on hook.

Example of 2-hdc dec

Double crochet decrease (dc dec): (Yo, insert hook, yo, draw lp through, yo, draw through 2 lps on hook) in each of the sts indicated, yo, draw through all lps on hook.

Example of 2-dc dec

US		UK
sl st (slip stitch)	=	sc (single crochet)
sc (single crochet)	=	dc (double crochet)
hdc (half double crochet)	=	htr (half treble crochet)
dc (double crochet)	=	tr (treble crochet)
tr (treble crochet)	=	dtr (double treble crochet)
dtr (double treble crochet)	=	ttr (triple treble crochet)
skip	=	miss

For more complete information, visit

StitchGuide.com